The Wildlife Trusts Guide to

BIRDS

The Wildlife Trusts Guide to
BIRDS

Series Editor Nicholas Hammond

Illustrated by
David Daly

NEW HOLLAND

First published in 2002 by
New Holland Publishers (UK) Ltd
Garfield House
86-88 Edgware Road
London W2 2EA
www.newhollandpublishers.com

10 9 8 7 6 5 4 3 2

This edition published in 2002 by
Advanced Marketing (UK) Ltd, Bicester, Oxfordshire

ISBN 1 84330 241 1

Publishing Manager: Jo Hemmings
Project Editor: Mike Unwin
Production: Joan Woodroffe
Bird Artwork: David Daly

Packaged by Wildlife Art Ltd:
www.wildlife-art.co.uk
Design and Cover Design: Sarah Crouch
Art/Copy Editor: Sarah Whittley
Proof-reading and Index: Rachel Lockwood

Reproduction by Modern Age
Repro Co. Ltd, Hong Kong
Printed and bound in Singapore by
Kyodo Printing Co (Singapore) Pte Ltd

Contents

Since 1912, The Wildlife Trusts have been speaking out for wildlife and undertaking practical action at the local level throughout the UK. Believing that wildlife is essential to a healthy environment for all, The Wildlife Trusts work with people from all walks of life – communities, industry, government, landowners, and families – to make sure nature gets a chance amongst all of the pressures of the modern world.

With years of experience and the service of the UK's top naturalists, The Wildlife Trusts and Wildlife Watch – the UK's leading club for young environmentalists – play a key part in restoring the balance between new developments and the natural world. With the specialist skills of volunteers and staff they manage more than 2,300 wildlife reserves (totalling more than 80,000 hectares), which are among the finest sites in the UK.

Their members, who number more than 340,000, contribute to their achievements by their generosity and hard work, and by spreading the message to everyone that wildlife matters.

The Wildlife Trusts is a registered charity (number 207238). For membership, and other details, please phone The Wildlife Trusts on 0870 0367711 or log on to www.wildlifetrusts.org

The most familiar class of animals in Britain and Ireland must be birds. Of the 10,000 or so species in the world there are about 420 European species. The species that appear in this book are arranged in an order that starts with the most primitive and finishes with the most highly developed. This classification is the result of years of study by ornithologists known as taxonomists, who study the relationship between animals and name them.

To classify animals, biologists divide them into a number of groups. Animals are divided into two main groups – invertebrates and vertebrates. The vertebrates have backbones and skeletons, namely fish, amphibians, reptiles, birds and mammals. Invertebrates, which may, like earthworms, have no hard parts or like insects, have a hard exoskeleton covering the soft parts of their bodies, cover every other class of animal. The next major category is the phylum, a very broad group and beneath that the class, which groups together all animals sharing similar characteristics: birds form a class of their own. Within each class there is a major division into orders: grebes are an example of an order of birds. The next important category is the family which includes all species that share certain characteristics: mice are a family within the order of rodents. Within each family the next category is the genus, grouping together similar species. The species is the group that contains all those individuals that have similar characteristics and which can produce fertile young.

Birds are distinguished from other classes of animal by having feathers, and have evolved from either dinosaurs or reptiles. Their front limbs have evolved into wings and their bones have become honeycombed with cells of air to provide the lightness necessary for flight. Great muscular strength is required to provide the lift necessary for flight and most birds have a deep keel-shaped breastbone that provides an anchor for the powerful wing muscles. A bird's body temperature is normally maintained at 38–40°C, which is 3–4°C warmer than most mammals.

Most of the species that visit gardens would be naturally found in woodland glades and edges, a habitat very similar to most gardens. However, if your garden pond contains fish, you may be visited by a kingfisher or grey heron. Larger ponds might attract moorhens, but the birds least likely to be seen in or over gardens are birds associated with water. Swimming birds have feet that are webbed or, like the grebes, are lobed with flattened pieces of skin on either side of each toe. Those that rarely venture on land have legs positioned towards the end of the body, because this enables them to swim underwater after their prey.

Those, like the mallard, are situated nearer the centre of the body, because as well as dabbling after food in water, they walk on land in search of food. A group of birds known as waders feed on the edge of water and long legs enable them to wade in the water searching for the invertebrates on which they feed. To make the most of the available food, species have evolved specially adapted bills: the oystercatcher has a thick bill that is strong enough to prise mussels and other shellfish from rocks, while the curlew has a long downwardly curving bill for probing deep mud for worms.

Looking at birds

Recognising birds means answering a number of questions. As you become more experienced you will be able to recognise some species very quickly and at a distance without even thinking about the questions.

How does it fly? What is its shape? Are there any distinguishing characteristics, such as the shape of the bill, the length of the tail, the length of the legs? What are the colours? Are there any characteristic plumage patterns? How does it behave? What noise does it make? Where is it? All these questions will help you to identify the species to which the bird belongs.

The flight of species or groups of birds can be a major clue to their identity. Woodland species such as woodpeckers have a distinctly undulating flight, which is particularly noticeable when they are flying across an open area. Kingfishers have a fast direct flight often close to the surface of water. The shape in flight may also be distinctive: ducks have pointed wings which move rapidly and necks that are outstretched. Experienced birdwatchers can differentiate species of ducks by their shapes and the way in which they fly.

Everyone knows what a duck looks like, but few people bother to think about how the shape differs from other types of bird. Compare the shape of a mallard with that of a mute swan. Both are waterbirds and have webbed feet, but the swan, unlike the mallard, rarely wanders far from water. Looking at shape is an important aid to identification.

Colour is not always a good guide, because the quality of light and the effect of local colour can cause variations that no book can cater for. The patterns of the plumage are probably more important. Since we often see birds flying away from us, it is important to know what their back views look like. Several species have distinctive tail patterns and wing-bars.

Behaviour of birds differs between species. Ducks for example can be divided into two groups depending on their feeding behaviour. One group dives beneath the surface to feed, while the other feeds from the surface. Therefore, look at the way the bird is feeding or relating to other birds. Many species are more likely to be seen in flocks, while others are usually seen singly. Some, such as the bullfinch, will frequently be seen in pairs.

The song, calls and other noises that birds make are obvious, if difficult, identification characteristics. Everyone is familiar with the call of the male cuckoo, a bird more often heard than seen, but how many of us can recognise the bubbling call of the female. The call of the kingfisher may be the first clue to its presence and the skulking nightingale is recognised far more frequently by its song than visually.

The best way to build your identification skills is to become familiar with the birds you see or hear often. This will give you a series of yardsticks with which to compare other species. If you know what a song thrush looks like, you will find it easier to identify a redwing when you see it, because you will notice the differences in the facial markings and the expression of the birds. Recognising calls and songs can be done in the same way. In other words, build up your portfolio of species. And if you can't recognise the species, you may still be able to identify the group to which it belongs.

The most important thing to remember is that birds are beautiful and fascinating animals. Enjoy looking at them.

Little grebe

Tachybaptus ruficollis

SIZE AND DESCRIPTION 27 cm long. The little grebe or dabchick in breeding plumage has bright chestnut cheeks and throat and dark brown upperparts. In winter it is grey, but still has the abrupt "powder-puff" rear. Sexes are similar.

VOICE Whinnying song.

HABITAT Still and slow-moving waters from ponds to rivers.

FOOD/HABITS Dives for food, mostly small fish. Rather skulking. Nests among waterside vegetation such as rushes or under overhanging branches.

Great crested grebe

Podiceps cristatus

SIZE AND DESCRIPTION 48 cm long. Unmistakable in breeding plumage, both sexes have a large horned crest and ruff. The head ornaments are lost in winter. Chicks are striped.

VOICE Generally silent. Call is usually a harsh bark; crooning song.

HABITAT Breeds on still waters, lakes, ponds and reservoirs, and slow-flowing rivers. It may be found on coasts and estuaries in winter.

FOOD/HABITS Dives for food, mostly fish and invertebrates, some plant matter. Often ingests feathers. Nests on a floating mat of reeds and other water plants, near the water's edge.

Fulmar

Fulmarus glacialis

SIZE AND DESCRIPTION 47 cm long. Seabird that resembles a gull, usually having grey upperparts and white underparts, but with rather thick neck. Wings held straight and stiff in flight. Nostrils in short tubes halfway down the bill.

VOICE Guttural chuckles and growls mainly at nest.

HABITAT Coasts, cliffs and sea.

FOOD/HABITS Eats fish, offal and molluscs. Nests in colonies on cliff faces. Returns to breeding sites November onwards, dispersing in late summer. Flight interspersed with frequent glides.

Gannet

Sula bassana

SIZE AND DESCRIPTION 90 cm long. Large all-white seabird. Wings are long and narrow with black tips, tail is pointed. Long, pointed blue-white bill. Yellow tinge to back of neck. Overall looks cigar-shaped. Juveniles are dark, becoming lighter as they mature at three years of age.

VOICE Harsh croaks at nest.

HABITAT Entirely maritime, only comes to land to breed.

FOOD/HABITS Diet almost exclusively fish, caught by spectacular arrow-shaped plunge-dives from heights of 15–30 m. Nests in dense colonies on cliffs and rocky islands.

Cormorant

Phalacrocorax carbo

SIZE AND DESCRIPTION 90 cm long. Very dark seabird with white throat and cheek patches, black-bronze upperparts, blue-black below. White thigh patch in breeding season. Swims low in water. On land "heraldic" pose with wings held out is characteristic. The sexes are similar; immature is brown.

VOICE At nest makes guttural noises.

HABITAT Present throughout the year on the coast; sometimes found inland on islands in lakes.

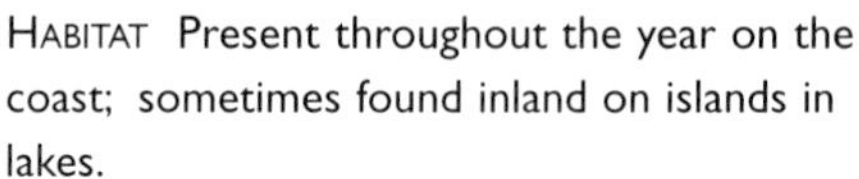

FOOD/HABITS Eats fish almost exclusively, which it catches by diving from the water surface. Nests in colonies, usually on rocks on the coast.

European race

juvenile

Grey heron

Ardea cinerea

SIZE AND DESCRIPTION 90–98 cm long. With its broad wings, slow, deep wing-beats, and legs stretched out behind, the grey heron looks very large in flight. Adults in breeding plumage have black crests, white necks and yellow bills. Juveniles are greyer and have darker bills.

VOICE Call is a harsh "frank".

HABITAT All types of waterways and wetlands. Will enter gardens, often early in morning, in search of fish. Widespread in Europe, except in the far north. Some birds move south during winter.

FOOD/HABITS Feeds on fish and other animals by waiting beside the water and striking with its strong bill.

Mute swan

Cygnus olor

SIZE AND DESCRIPTION 152 cm long. Largest flying bird. Resident. Adults are all white; immatures are grey-brown. Told from wintering bewick's and whooper swans by orange bill with black knob at base (smaller in female) and more graceful curve to neck.

VOICE Generally silent, it hisses when angry or disturbed.

HABITAT Almost any still or slow-moving inland water body, also estuaries and sheltered coastal regions.

FOOD/HABITS Usually feeds on water by dipping neck below surface, sometimes up-ending.

Greylag goose

Anser anser

SIZE AND DESCRIPTION 83 cm long. Large grey goose with orange bill and flesh-coloured legs.

VOICE Calls in flight "aahng-ung-ung".

HABITAT The flow country, marshy moorland during the breeding season. A winter visitor to saltmarsh and fresh marshes, grasslands and estuaries.

FOOD/HABITS Diet is mostly grass but also takes cereals in autumn and winter. Feral birds present all year, but wild birds are mostly winter visitors to Great Britain.

Canada goose

Branta canadensis

SIZE AND DESCRIPTION 97 cm long. A species introduced to Great Britain, it is now common and widespread. A large grey-brown goose, with black head and neck and white patch on chin, extending up head. Distinguished from barnacle and brent geese by larger size, longer neck, and preference for inland habitats.

VOICE Loud trumpet-like call "ah-honk".

HABITAT Inland waters, including park lakes and ponds. Also found on coasts and marshes during winter.

FOOD/HABITS Feeds mainly on grass.

Shelduck

Tadorna tadorna

SIZE AND DESCRIPTION 61 cm long. Large duck with bold markings: head and neck are dark green, wide chestnut breast band, black on wingtips and end of tail, white underparts. The sexes are similar.

VOICE Generally silent, but drake can give whistle in flight. Female quacks.

HABITAT Estuaries, sandy shores and saltmarshes.

FOOD/HABITS Feeds chiefly on small molluscs caught by sweeping bill through soft estuarine mud. Nests in dunes in rabbit burrows.

Wigeon

Anas penelope

SIZE AND DESCRIPTION 18 cm long. The drake has a chestnut head, with creamy yellow stripe from bill over the crown, pinkish breast, short blue, black-tipped bill. Green speculum. White patches on wings are visible in flight.

VOICE Drake has a whistling "whee-oo" call.

HABITAT Marshes. Winters throughout Great Britain, often on coastal marshes and estuaries, but also inland.

FOOD/HABITS Eats mostly plant matter, which it takes from the water surface. It is often seen in flocks grazing on land.

Mallard

Anas platyrhynchos

SIZE AND DESCRIPTION 58 cm long. Our commonest duck. The drake has a dark, rich brown breast, dark green head with white collar. Speculum is purple.

VOICE Ducks give the familiar "quack", drake has a higher-pitched call.

HABITAT Resident and widespread, the mallard can be found on almost any inland water other than fast-flowing rivers. Often more coastal in winter.

FOOD/HABITS Surface feeding, it can be seen dabbling and up-ending. It eats a variety of food, including invertebrates, fish and plants. Nests usually on the ground under bushes, close to water.

Teal

Anas crecca

SIZE AND DESCRIPTION 35 cm long. Smaller, neater appearance than mallard. Drake has chestnut head with green eye-stripe, speckled breast, creamy undertail. Green speculum.

VOICE Drake gives a whistling "crrick, crrick" call.

HABITAT Prefers still or slow-moving fresh water, with dense fringing vegetation. Resident throughout Great Britain.

FOOD/HABITS A dabbling duck, it eats mostly plants and seeds. It may nest som distance from water. Fast in flight; springs up from water.

Shoveler

Anas clypeata

SIZE AND DESCRIPTION 51 cm long. Surface-feeding duck, easily recognised by very large, spatulate bill. Drake has dark green head, white breast, chestnut flanks. Forewing is blue. Green speculum.

VOICE Drake calls "took-took"; females "quack".

HABITAT Lakes, reservoirs; likes creeks, reeds, marshy areas with plenty of cover.

FOOD/HABITS Feeds in shallow, muddy water, sieves seeds through its bill.

Pochard

Aythya ferina

SIZE AND DESCRIPTION 46 cm long. Drake has chestnut head, black breast and grey back and flanks. Light-blue bill. Female is brown with a pale throat.

VOICE A quiet bird; male gives a soft whistle, female growls.

HABITAT Large ponds, lakes, slow-flowing streams, with fringing vegetation. Outside the breeding season it can be seen on a wide range of fresh water bodies.

FOOD/HABITS Diving duck, more active at night and often seen resting on water by day.

Tufted duck

Aythya fuligula

SIZE AND DESCRIPTION 43 cm long. Jaunty little diving duck. Drake is black and white with drooping crest on back of head; duck is dark brown with suggestion of crest. The bill is blue with a dark tip.

VOICE Tends to be silent.

HABITAT Medium-sized or large fresh waters with fringing vegetation. More widespread in winter when it will occur on more open gravel pits and reservoirs without cover.

FOOD/HABITS Dives deeper than pochard, eating mostly insects and molluscs. Nests on the ground within a few metres of the water's edge.

Osprey

Pandion haliaetus

SIZE AND DESCRIPTION 55 cm long. Large, graceful bird of prey with dark brown upperparts and white underparts. Long narrow wings held angled in flight. Summer visitor.
VOICE Call is a short, shrill whistle.
HABITAT Lakes, lochs and rivers; reservoirs on passage.
FOOD/HABITS Feeds on fish, which it catches usually by plunge-diving from a height of 10–30 m. Flies holding fish in its talons in line with its own head and tail. Nests in tall trees in Scandinavia and Scotland. Elsewhere, mostly a passage migrant.

Black kite

Milvus migrans

SIZE AND DESCRIPTION 56 cm long. All dark bird of prey with slightly forked tail, squarer than that of red kite.

VOICE Rather noisy, has a high-pitched squeal.

HABITAT Hunts over water, but found in most habitats, including towns except woodland.

FOOD/HABITS Feeds largely on carrion. Gregarious. Widespread in southern Europe. Occurs as a rare vagrant in Great Britain.

Red kite

Milvus milvus

SIZE AND DESCRIPTION 61 cm long. Grey head, russet above and below, with white patch on underwing and deeply forked tail, twisted and turned in flight.

VOICE Mewing call, higher-pitched than buzzard's.

HABITAT Deciduous woodland and open countryside.

FOOD/HABITS Eats chiefly earthworms, also mammals (especially rabbits), birds and carrion. Nests in trees. A rare resident, breeding birds are mostly confined to Wales, but young birds wander far and wide.

Buzzard

Buteo buteo

SIZE AND DESCRIPTION 51–56 cm long. Large bird of prey with broad rounded wings and proportionately short tail. Usually dark brown above with variable amounts of white below, sometimes with a dark carpal patch.

VOICE Mewing cry "peeioo".

HABITAT A resident, but more common in the west and north of the country, the buzzard prefers moorland and agricultural land.

FOOD/HABITS It feeds mainly on small mammals, particularly rabbits, which it catches with a low-flying pounce. Also eats carrion. Direct flight may be rather ponderous but it can often be seen soaring and spiralling, and sometimes hovers when hunting.

Marsh harrier

Circus aeruginosus

SIZE AND DESCRIPTION 52 cm long. Largest European harrier, summer visitor. It is usually dark brown above, with buff shoulders and head. Male has grey tail and grey secondaries. Often flies with wings held in shallow "V".

VOICE Two-note display call "kweeoo".

HABITAT Reedbeds and marshes.

FOOD/HABITS Eats small mammals, frogs and birds and their eggs. Hunts by systematically quartering the ground. Nests in reedbeds.

Sparrowhawk

Accipiter nisus

SIZE AND DESCRIPTION 28–38 cm long. Wings are blunt and broad. Males, which are much smaller than females, have blue-grey heads and backs, and breasts barred with rusty-red. Females have grey-brown barring on their breasts and a pale "eyebrow".

VOICE Makes a monotonous ringing call near the nest.

HABITAT Woodland, parks, gardens and hedgerows. Breeds across Europe, but British populations are mainly resident.

FOOD/HABITS Small birds are the main food of sparrowhawks, which hunt by ambushing their prey.

Kestrel

Falco tinnunculus

SIZE AND DESCRIPTION 33–39 cm long. Distinctive long tail and pointed wings. Males have grey heads, black-tipped grey tails and dark-flecked russet backs. Females and juveniles lack the grey head, have brown tails with narrow bars and have more dark flecks on their backs.

VOICE Kestrels are noisy at the nest-site, with their rasping "kee-kee-kee-kee" call.

HABITAT Farmland, moorland and other open areas. Breeds in cities and towns, and may be seen flying over gardens. Resident across Europe, although north- and east-European populations migrate during autumn.

FOOD/HABITS Hovers above grassland or perches on trees and pylons, ready to drop down on rodents in the grass. Also feeds on small birds, large insects and lizards.

Hobby

Falco subbuteo

SIZE AND DESCRIPTION 30–36 cm long. A summer visitor to Great Britain. Dashing little falcon that looks like a large swift in flight. Dark, slaty-grey above with dark moustache on white cheeks and throat, and red thighs.

VOICE A clear, repeated "kew-kew-kew".

HABITAT Mostly heathlands, where it often nests in pine trees.

FOOD/HABITS Feeds on small birds, and large insects such as dragonflies that are often eaten in flight.

Grey partridge

Perdix perdix

SIZE AND DESCRIPTION 30 cm long. Grey-brown upper and underparts, male with horse-shoe shaped chestnut patch on breast. Whirring flight.

VOICE Loud "kar-wit, kar-wit", rapid cackling when it is startled into flight.
HABITAT Farmland, especially cereals and arable with patches of longer vegetation, open country, moorland and heath, becoming increasingly rare.
FOOD/HABITS Eats mainly seeds, cereals, flower buds, but also takes insects. Insects are particularly important food for chicks. Substantial population decline attributed to use of herbicides. Unsprayed headlands improve chick survival rates.

Red-legged partridge

Alectoris rufa

SIZE AND DESCRIPTION 34 cm long. A little larger than native grey partridge, the red-legged is an introduced species. White cheeks and throat, flanks barred with white, black and chestnut, red bill and legs separate it from grey partridge.
VOICE Harsh "chucka, chucka".
HABITAT Open country and farmland, found in rather drier areas than grey partridge.
FOOD/HABITS Mainly eats seeds and plant matter. Nests on the ground among grass or tall vegetation or under a bush.

Pheasant

Phasianus colchicus

SIZE AND DESCRIPTION Male is 75–90 cm long; female 53–64 cm. Males have long, golden, barred tails, green heads and red wattles. Some may have white rings around their necks. Females have shorter tails and are buffish-brown.

VOICE Gives a loud, hoarse metallic call.

HABITAT Woodlands, farmland with hedges, big gardens and reedbeds. Introduced to Greece from Asia 2,000 years ago, and now spread across much of Europe.

FOOD/HABITS Feeds on seeds, fruit, nuts and roots.

Coot

Fulica atra

SIZE AND DESCRIPTION 38 cm long. All-black waterbird with white bill and shield on forehead. Greenish legs. Domed back. Favours more open water than moorhen. Chicks are black with rufous heads; the juveniles are greyish.

VOICE Quite noisy, call is usually a loud "kowk" or variation.

HABITAT Occurs on still and slow-moving fresh water. Found on larger water bodies than moorhen.

FOOD/HABITS Dives for food, largely aquatic plants. Often in flocks especially outside the breeding season. Requires fringing vegetation for nesting. Quarrelsome; coots fight on the water using their large feet.

Moorhen

Gallinula chloropus

SIZE AND DESCRIPTION 32–35 cm long. With its slaty plumage, very dark brown wings, white undertail coverts, yellow-tipped red bill and green legs, the moorhen is unmistakable. It flicks its tail as it walks with a careful tread. When swimming, its head jerks forward and its tail points upwards, giving the body a triangular appearance. Young birds are brown.

VOICE The varied repertoire includes harsh metallic "krrek" and "kittick" calls.

HABITAT Ponds, rivers, canals, lakes and marshes across Europe. Also found in parks and gardens with large ponds.

FOOD/HABITS Moorhens are omnivores, feeding on seeds, insects, molluscs, leaves and carrion.

Snipe

Gallinago gallinago

SIZE AND DESCRIPTION 27 cm long. Wader most likely to be seen when flushed, flying off in zigzag fashion. Extremely long bill, striped yellow and dark brown head and upperparts.

VOICE Hoarse cry when flushed.

HABITAT Flood meadows, grasslands, marshlands and bogs.

FOOD/HABITS Eats mainly worms but also molluscs, insects and other invertebrates. Most active at dawn and dusk. Display flight involves 45 degree dive, with bleating noise caused by air rushing through outspread tail feathers.

Woodcock

Scolopax rusticola

SIZE AND DESCRIPTION 34 cm long. Steep pale forehead, long bill, laterally striped crown, marbled brown and buff upperparts. Most likely to be seen in display flight, "roding", at dawn and dusk.

VOICE Call given in display flight, a croak followed by "tsiwick".

HABITAT Woodland with wet, swampy areas and open glades and rides as well as dense undergrowth cover.

FOOD/HABITS Diet mostly worms, also insects and larvae, seeds and grass. Crepuscular.

Avocet

Recurvirostra avosetta

SIZE AND DESCRIPTION 43 cm long. Large, elegant, boldly marked black-and-white wader, with black crown and nape, blue-grey legs, and slender up-turned bill.

VOICE Call a liquid "kluut".

HABITAT Saltmarsh, brackish lagoons and mudflats.

FOOD/HABITS Feeds chiefly on shrimp-like crustaceans, ragworms, other invertebrates and fish spawn. Distinctive feeding method of vigorous sideways swishes of bill through water and silty mud. Mainly a summer visitor with breeding largely confined to coastal nature reserves in East Anglia and south-east England. Over winter south-west and western Africa. In mild winters, many stay in western Europe.

Oystercatcher

Haematopus ostralegus

SIZE AND DESCRIPTION 43 cm long. A large, boldly marked black and white wader with orange-red bill and pink legs. White rump and wing bar. White collar in winter.

VOICE A noisy bird with loud "kleep" call and piping display.

HABITAT Generally coastal, where it breeds on seashores, shingle banks, also on uplands.

FOOD/HABITS Eats mainly invertebrates, especially molluscs, which it opens by hammering or prising (some oystercatchers have pointed bills, others have squarer-ended bills). Resident throughout the year, also a passage migrant and winter visitor. Nests on the ground.

Lapwing

Vanellus vanellus

SIZE AND DESCRIPTION 30 cm long. Dark glossy metallic green upperparts, white below with buff undertail, long wispy crest. Throat black in breeding season. Immature has short crest. Looks pied in flight.

VOICE Calls "peewit".

HABITAT Farmland, grassland, moorland and marshes; also coasts and estuaries in winter.

FOOD/HABITS Diet is mostly invertebrates; insects, worms and molluscs, with some vegetable matter. Nests on the ground. Floppy, loose, broad-winged flight. Tumbling display flight by males in spring. Winter flocks may be mixed with golden plovers.

Ringed plover

Charadrius hiaticula

SIZE AND DESCRIPTION 19 cm long. Common shorebird with black mask and breast band, white collar and forehead. Upperparts brown, underparts white. Narrow white wing bar. The black markings are more subdued in winter.

VOICE Calls are a liquid "tooi" and "kluup". Trilling song.

HABITAT Seashores, sandy and muddy shores in winter.

FOOD/HABITS Mainly eats insects, worms and molluscs, some plant matter.

Golden plover

Pluvialis apricaria

SIZE AND DESCRIPTION 28 cm long. Resident. Breeding plumage is spangled yellow and brown, with black throat and belly, northern birds being more boldly marked. Outside the breeding season the black on the underparts is absent.

VOICE A liquid whistling call "tlui". Song is liquid "too-roo, too-roo".

HABITAT Upland moorland. Flocks in winter on farmland.

FOOD/HABITS Eats mostly insects, molluscs, and some plant matter.

Dunlin

Calidris alpina

SIZE AND DESCRIPTION 17–19 cm long. Slightly smaller than sanderling, with longer bill, less conspicuous white wing bar. Summer plumage is scaly black and brown above, white below with large black belly patch. In winter it is greyer with a whitish belly.

VOICE Call in flight "treep".

HABITAT Upland moorland, marshes and bogs. Outside the breeding season, seashores, mudflats, creeks and estuaries, but it also visits inland waters.

FOOD/HABITS Feeds on small invertebrates, such as molluscs and worms.

Sanderling

Calidris alba

SIZE AND DESCRIPTION 20 cm long. Pale grey in winter plumage. Summer plumage is scaly brown above and on breast, with white belly shows white wing bar in all plumages.

VOICE In flight, liquid "twick, twick".

HABITAT Breeds farther north than Great Britain. Occurs as passage migrant and winter visitor, where it is confined to the coast.

FOOD/HABITS Distinctive feeding method as it runs in and out on the shore with the movement of the waves, often likened to a clockwork toy.

Knot

Calidris canutus

SIZE AND DESCRIPTION 25 cm long. A winter visitor to our coasts and shores. A little larger than dunlin, with comparatively short bill. Winter plumage is grey. Narrow white wing bar. Breeding plumage rufous.

VOICE Call "knut".

HABITAT Coasts and shores, estuaries and mudflats.

FOOD/HABITS Feeds on invertebrates such as insects, molluscs, earthworms and crustaceans. Usually seen in flocks, which can be very large and dense. Spectacular aerial maneouvres as flocks come in to roost at high tide.

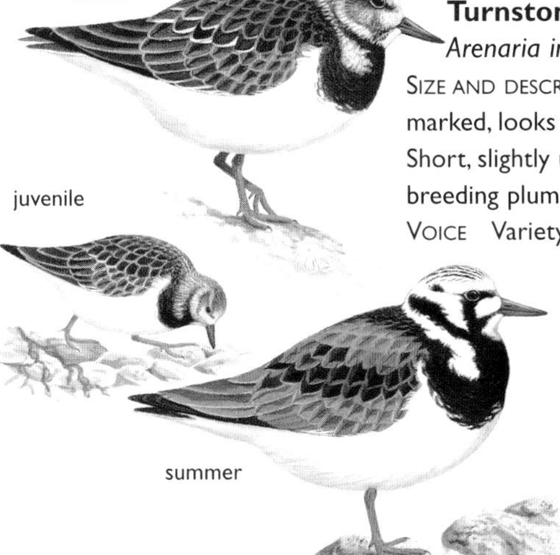

Turnstone

Arenaria interpres

SIZE AND DESCRIPTION 23 cm long. Boldly marked, looks blacks and white, winter visitor. Short, slightly upturned bill. Rufous markings in breeding plumage give tortoiseshell appearance.

VOICE Variety of calls. Typically short and nasal.

HABITAT Seashores, with rocks and pebbles, also sandflats and mudflats.

FOOD/HABITS Diet is mainly insects, molluscs, crustaceans, which it finds by using its bill to overturn pebbles, and pieces of seaweed.

Wood sandpiper

Tringa glareola

SIZE AND DESCRIPTION 20 cm long. Size and plumage similar to green sandpiper, but longer legged and more delicate. Upperparts mottled brownish-grey with distinct spotting and clear feather edges. Juvenile slightly darker.

VOICE A dry "chiff if if".

HABITAT Freshwater marshes and flooded meadows.

FOOD/HABITS Wades in shallow water, feeds on invertebrates and plants.

Common sandpiper

Actitis hypoleucos

SIZE AND DESCRIPTION 20 cm long. Small wader with brown upperparts, white underparts, white sides to rump and tail and white wing bar.

VOICE Call in flight "twee-wee-wee". Song more melodious.

HABITAT Upland streams and lochs. Non breeding season it occurs on passage on inland waters such as reservoirs, sewage farms, and coastal areas.

FOOD/HABITS Eats mainly invertebrates, some plant matter. Flicks tail.

Black-tailed godwit

Limosa limosa

SIZE AND DESCRIPTION 41 cm long. Breeding plumage has rufous-coloured breast. Colour outside breeding season is grey-brown. In flight, broad white wingbar and white band on tail above black band distinguishes this species from bar-tailed godwit.
VOICE Call in flight "wicka-wicka-wicka". Song "crweetuu".
HABITAT Grassland and flood meadows. Outside the breeding season, occurs on coastal areas.
FOOD/HABITS Feeds mostly on insects and larvae, also molluscs and worms.

Bar-tailed godwit

Limosa lapponica

SIZE AND DESCRIPTION 37 cm long. Shorter legged and more robust than black-tailed. In flight distinct white rump and barred tail.
VOICE Flight call nasal, similar to knot's.
HABITAT Winters on tidal mudflats and sandy shores, also grassland. Breeds Scandinavia and tundra.
FOOD/HABITS Probes mud for crabs, shrimps and marine worms in winter, insects taken mainly in summer.

winter

summer

Redshank

Tringa totanus

SIZE AND DESCRIPTION 28 cm long. Grey-brown wading bird with orange-red bill and legs. Plumage greyer in winter. White rump and trailing edges to wings noticeable in flight.

VOICE Variety of yelping calls. Song "tu-udle..." may be given in flight or from the ground.

HABITAT Breeds on flood meadows, grassland and lowland moors both near the coast and inland. Winters on coast, especially estuaries and mudflats. More widespread on passage.

FOOD/HABITS Feeds mostly on invertebrates. Often perches conspicuously on posts.

Greenshank

Tringa nebularia

SIZE AND DESCRIPTION 30.5 cm long. A rather pale, grey wader. The legs are green. In flight it shows a white tail, rump and lower back.

VOICE Lower pitched call than redshank. Song "ru-tu, ru-tu ..." given in flight or while perched.

HABITAT Summers in northern moorland. Otherwise, riverbanks, marshes and estuaries.

FOOD/HABITS Feeds almost entirely on invertebrates, amphibians and fish.

Curlew

Numenius arquata

SIZE AND DESCRIPTION 53–58 cm long. Largest wader with very long, decurved bill. Plumage streaked brown. Bigger and more robust than whimbrel. White "V" shape on rump shows in flight.

VOICE Distinctive, liquid call "coor-wee".

HABITAT Uplands; moorland and pasture. More coastal in winter, feeding on mudflats, estuaries and seashores.

FOOD/HABITS Long bill enables it to probe mud and sand deeply. Eats mainly small invertebrates, fish and plant matter. Present all year. Occurs in flocks outside the breeding season but feeds more separately.

Whimbrel

Numenius phaeopus

SIZE AND DESCRIPTION 41 cm long. Smaller and more slender than curlew, with shorter bill and markedly striped face, pale crown stripe and dark stripe above eye. White "V" shape on rump shows in flight.

VOICE Has a liquid bubbling call.

HABITAT Mostly a passage migrant to Great Britain, stopping on the shores and coasts en route to wintering grounds farther south.

FOOD/HABITS Eats mostly molluscs, worms and crustaceans. Nests on the ground.

Black-headed gull

Larus ridibundus

SIZE AND DESCRIPTION 35–39 cm long. Most likely to be seen in winter, when the head is white with a grey-brown crescent behind the eye. Immature birds, whose backs and heads are mottled with cream and brown, moult into adult plumage over two years. In breeding plumage, both sexes develop a chocolate-brown head. Note the bill, which is red and finer than most other European gulls.

VOICE Noisy when in flocks. Calls include a strident "kee-yah".

HABITAT Breeds in colonies on moorland bogs, reedbeds, freshwater marshes and lakes across northern Europe. In winter, it is common on ploughed fields, town parks, playing fields, large gardens and coasts. Russian and east-European populations migrate south-west during winter.

FOOD/HABITS Feeds on invertebrates, seeds and scavenges among rubbish.

Common gull

Larus canus

SIZE AND DESCRIPTION 41 cm long. Resembles a small herring gull, but note yellow-green legs and lack of red spot on bill. Grey upperparts, white below, black wingtips, "kind" facial expression. Immatures are streaked brown.
VOICE Higher pitched than the large gulls.
HABITAT Coasts; breeds on moorland, freshwater lochs.
FOOD/HABITS Earthworms, insects, seeds, small mammals, birds, marine invertebrates. Nests on the ground. Mainly resident in Britain with winter visitors from northern Europe. After breeding many move south.

Herring gull

Larus argentatus

SIZE AND DESCRIPTION 61 cm long. Silver-grey upperparts, black wingtips, white head and underparts, yellow bill with red spot, pink legs. In winter head and neck streaked brown.
VOICE Wide variety of wailing calls. Loudest is "kyow-kyow-kyow".
HABITAT Coasts, and in shore waters.
FOOD/HABITS Varied diet; fish, crustaceans, carrion and birds.

adult

juveniles

Lesser black-backed gull

Larus fuscus

SIZE AND DESCRIPTION 55 cm long. Dark grey back, white head and underparts, yellow bill with red spot, yellow legs. Immature is brown, slightly darker than herring gull.
VOICE Loud calls, deeper than herring gull's.
HABITAT Coasts and sea. May breed on inland fresh waters.
FOOD/HABITS Eats almost anything; fish, small mammals, birds and their eggs and carrion. May feed at rubbish tips.

Great black-backed gull

Larus marinus

SIZE AND DESCRIPTION 72 cm. Very large gull, black upperparts, white head and underparts, yellow bill with red spot, pink legs. Brown in winter. Immature is brown.
VOICE Deep hoarse calls "uk-uk-uk".
HABITAT Coasts and islands during breeding season. At other times also on estuaries and inland fresh waters.
FOOD/HABITS Eats a wide variety of creatures, including fish, birds, mammals and carrion. May feed at rubbish tips.

Kittiwake

Rissa tridactyla

SIZE AND DESCRIPTION 41 cm long. Small gull with grey back and wings, white head and underparts, dark eye, yellow bill and black legs. Solid black wingtips separate it from common gull, which has white "windows". Immature has dark "W" shape across wingspan.

VOICE Calls its own name "kitt-ee-wayke".

HABITAT Cliff-breeding, otherwise almost entirely marine.

FOOD/HABITS Feeds on fish, worms, molluscs and crustaceans. Nests in colonies, on cliff ledges.

Sandwich tern

Sterna sandvicensis

SIZE AND DESCRIPTION 41 cm. Largest tern, with whiter plumage, relatively shorter tail and heavier bill. Breeding adults have black crown with shaggy crest, black legs and black bill with yellow tip. White forehead in winter.

VOICE Distinctive, harsh "kirrick".

HABITAT An almost exclusively maritime species.

FOOD/HABITS Fish and other marine invertebrates. Nests in crowded colonies on sand or shingle banks.

Common tern

Sterna hirundo

SIZE AND DESCRIPTION 35 cm long. Mostly a summer visitor. Grey upperparts, black crown, dark red legs and bill, which has a black tip. Long forked tail. White forehead in winter.

VOICE Call is a strident "keeyah" and "wik-kik-kik".

HABITAT Breeds on islands, inshore waters near low-lying coasts and gravel pits. On passage occurs on lakes, inland waters.

FOOD/HABITS Eats fish, worms, insects. molluscs, crustaceans. Often dives for fish. Nests on dunes, saltmarsh, shingle banks, in colonies.

juvenile

summer

Arctic tern

Sterna paradisaea

SIZE AND DESCRIPTION 35 cm long. Generally seen on passage. Similar to common tern, but with blood-red bill. In winter, white forehead with black bill. Tends to have longer tail streamers.

VOICE Calls similar to common tern, also a high whistling "kee, kee".

HABITAT More maritime than common tern.

FOOD/HABITS Eats fish, insects, molluscs, crustaceans.

Guillemot

Uria aalge

SIZE AND DESCRIPTION 43 cm long. Member of the auk family. Has short stubby wings, pied plumage and short legs. Guillemot's upperparts are black/brown. Some birds have a white line over the eye and are known as "bridled". Winter, throat is white.

VOICE Call is a caw "aargh".

HABITAT Breeds on seacliffs, otherwise totally marine.

FOOD/HABITS Eats fish and other marine animals. Lays eggs straight onto narrow cliff ledges.

Razorbill

Alca torda

SIZE AND DESCRIPTION 41 cm long. Black and white, strong vertically flattened bill. Immatures and winter birds have a white throat.

VOICE Makes a whirring sound and growls.

HABITAT Breeds on seacliffs; winters at sea.

FOOD/HABITS Diet is almost entirely marine creatures. Fish are caught by diving from the water surface and pursued underwater by flapping wings like flippers. Flight fast and whirring, usually low over water.

Puffin

Fratercula arctica

SIZE AND DESCRIPTION 30 cm long. Instantly recognisable by its brightly coloured bill and clown-like face markings. Smaller than both razorbill and guillemot. In winter bill is smaller and greyer, and face is smudged.

VOICE Growling "aar".

HABITAT Clifftops and islands with grassy slopes where it nests in rabbit burrows. At sea during winter.

FOOD/HABITS Eats mainly fish, especially sand-eels, capable of holding several at same time in notched bill. Highly gregarious.

Collared dove

Streptopelia decaocto

SIZE AND DESCRIPTION 31–33 cm long. Slimmer than other pigeons. The back is brown buff, while the head and underparts are pinkish-brown. There is a black ring around nape of neck, and the wings have whitish undersides.

VOICE A rapidly repeated "koo-koo, koo".

HABITAT Towns, gardens and farmland with hedges. Has spread across Europe from Asia.

FOOD/HABITS Feeds on seeds and grain. A frequent bird-table visitor. Large flocks assemble at grain stores.

Feral pigeon

Columba livia

SIZE AND DESCRIPTION 31–33 cm long. With black wing-bars and a white rump, many feral pigeons resemble the rock doves from which they originate. But colours may vary from white to very dark grey, and some may be pale fawn.

VOICE A soft cooing.

HABITAT Sea cliffs, towns and villages.

FOOD/HABITS Seeds, grain and discarded human food.

Stock dove

Columba oenas

SIZE AND DESCRIPTION 32–34 cm long. Smaller and less chunky than the woodpigeon, with a noticeable black trailing edge to the black-tipped wings. It lacks the wingbars and white rump of the feral pigeon.
VOICE A monotonously repeated "roo-roo-oo".
HABITAT Woods and farmland, parks and gardens. Breeds across Europe. Absent from Iceland.
FOOD/HABITS Feeds on seeds and grain, often in flocks with wood pigeons.

Woodpigeon

Columba palumbus

SIZE AND DESCRIPTION Measuring 40–42 cm long, this is the largest European pigeon. Adults have white rings around the neck, and a white bar across each wing. The wings make a clattering sound on take-off and landing.
VOICE A soft, often repeated "coo-coo-coo-cu-coo".
HABITAT Woodland, farmland, parks and gardens. Found across Europe.
FOOD/HABITS Eats seeds, berries and beechmast. Feeds in flocks throughout the winter.

Cuckoo

Cuculus canorus

SIZE AND DESCRIPTION 32–38 cm long. Grey, with a pale, barred breast. Some females may be rufous. Immature birds are barred, brown, with a white patch on the nape. This slim-looking bird has long, sweptback wings and a long, rounded tail. It often settles on trees, telegraph wires, large bushes or fence posts, perching with a cocked tail and drooping wings.

VOICE Males give the well-known "cuckoo" call. Females have a bubbling trill.

HABITAT Found in a wide range of habitats, including moorland, heathland, open woodland, parks and large gardens. The cuckoo is a summer visitor to all of Europe except Iceland. It arrives from Africa in April and leaves in late summer.

FOOD/HABITS Eats insects and is capable of swallowing hairy caterpillars. Females lay eggs in other birds' nests.

Tawny owl

Strix aluco

SIZE AND DESCRIPTION 38 cm long. Woodland owl, more likely to be heard than seen as almost entirely nocturnal. Brown plumage, broad rounded wings, feathered feet, dark eyes, round face mask.

VOICE Song, familiar hooting "hoo, hoo"; call is a sharp "'kewick".

HABITAT Deciduous woodland, town parks.

FOOD/HABITS Mostly eats small mammals such as woodmice, and small birds. May be betrayed at roost in daylight by small birds mobbing. Nests in holes in trees.

Little owl

Athene noctua

SIZE AND DESCRIPTION 22 cm long. Introduced species, now widespread in England. More likely to be seen in daylight than tawny or barn owl. Yellow eyes, "fierce" expression, long legs, brown upper parts spotted with white.

VOICE Call a ringing "kiew, kiew".

HABITAT Open country, farmland, with scattered trees. Open woodland.

FOOD/HABITS Diet is chiefly large insects and other invertebrates, such as worms. Nests in holes in trees.

Barn owl

Tyto alba

SIZE AND DESCRIPTION 34 cm long. Golden spangled back, white heart-shaped face and white underparts. Largely nocturnal, often seen in car headlights as it searches verges for prey. Longer wings and legs than tawny owl.

VOICE Call is a screech, also makes hissing and snoring sounds.

HABITAT Needs open country with rough grassland for hunting.

FOOD/HABITS Feeds mainly on rodents especially rats and voles. Nests in buildings, usually old barns and farm outhouses.

Kingfisher

Alcedo atthis

SIZE AND DESCRIPTION 17–19.5 cm long. Although brightly coloured, the kingfisher is well camouflaged when perched among autumn leaves. The bill is black, but breeding females have a reddish base to the lower mandible. Juveniles have a pale spot at the tip of the bill.

VOICE A distinctive whistle.

HABITAT Rivers, streams and lakes. Will visit garden ponds to take small ornamental fish.

FOOD/HABITS Fish are the main food. The kingfisher hunts by diving into the water from a perch or by hovering and then diving.

Hoopoe

Upupa epops

SIZE AND DESCRIPTION 25–29 cm long. Upper parts are sandy-fawn, with black-and-white barred wings and tail. The bill curves downwards. The hoopoe's crest is raised momentarily when the bird lands. The wings are broad and the flight is flappy, often low over the ground. It walks jerkily, with a starling-like gait.

VOICE A repeated "poo-poo-poo".

HABITAT Gardens, vineyards, olive groves, and farmland with bushes. The hoopoe visits northern Europe between late April and September, moving south to North Africa and southern Spain in winter.

FOOD/HABITS Insects, worms and small reptiles.

Great spotted woodpecker

Dendrocopos major

SIZE AND DESCRIPTION 23–26 cm long. A blackbird-sized, black-and-white bird. It has white shoulder patches, with red under the tail. The male has red patch on the nape, while the female's nape is black. Juvenile has a red crown. Flight is undulating. Similar species include the lesser spotted woodpecker, which is sparrow-sized.

VOICE A short, sharp "tchak" call, which may be repeated at 1-second intervals. In spring, it drums very fast on rotten branches.

HABITAT All kinds of woodland, large gardens and parks.

FOOD/HABITS Insects and grubs, and conifer seeds in winter. Will visit garden feeders. Also steals eggs and young from other birds' nests.

Green woodpecker

Picus viridis

SIZE AND DESCRIPTION 30–36 cm. Green plumage, but the adult has a distinctive yellow rump and red cap. Juveniles are speckled, and appear more grey. Flight is deeply undulating. The pale eye, black face and moustachial stripe give the bird a "fierce" appearance. The male has a red centre to the moustachial stripe, while the female's is black.

VOICE An unmistakable shrill, laughing call. Rarely drums.

HABITAT Open and mixed woodlands, farmland, parkland and large gardens.

FOOD/HABITS Feeds on insect grubs and ants, for which it probes rotten wood and soil. It is often seen feeding on lawns and decaying timber.

Swift

Apus apus

SIZE AND DESCRPTION 17 cm long. The swift has long, narrow, crescent-shaped wings, a torpedo-shaped body and a short forked tail. It has a dark brown plumage with a pale throat.

VOICE A shrill, monotone scream, which is often uttered by tight flocks flying round buildings at roof-top height.

HABITAT Breeds in towns and villages, but feeds in the sky, often several kilometres from nest-sites. A summer visitor to northern Europe (except Iceland), usually arriving in May and leaving in August.

FOOD/HABITS The swift is adapted to feed on high-flying insects, which it catches in its wide, gaping mouth. It has very short legs and shuffles around its nest-site. Most of its life is spent on the wing.

Swallow

Hirundo rustica

SIZE AND DESCRIPTION 17–22 cm long, including a tail of 3–6.5 cm. Juveniles are slightly smaller. The swallow's wings are long and pointed, and its tail deeply forked. It has pale cream underparts, dark blue wings and back, and a red throat with a blue-black neck band. Flight is fast, with powerful wingbeats.

VOICE In flight, it has a high-pitched "vit-vit" call. The warning call for cats (and other ground predators) is a sharp "sifflit"; for birds of prey it is a "flitt-flitt". The song is a rapid, rattling twitter.

HABITAT Breeds in farmyards and small-village gardens with surrounding open country. Often seen near water. It is a summer visitor to northern Europe, arriving in late March and April, and leaving in September and October.

FOOD/HABITS Feeds on insects, which it catches in flight by flying low over fields and water.

House martin

Delichon urbica

SIZE AND DESCRIPTION 12.5 cm long. Wings are broader than the swallow's and the forked tail is shorter, giving the house martin a stubbier appearance. The rump is white, while the wings, head and tail are dark blue. Flight is more fluttery than the swallow's, and flaps are often interspersed with glides. Underparts of juveniles tend to be a duskier white than on adults.

VOICE A harsh twitter. Song is a series of formless chirps.

HABITAT Breeds in colonies in towns and villages, and cliffs.

FOOD/HABITS Tends to feed on flying insects at a greater altitude than the swallow. Rarely seen on the ground, except when collecting mud for its nest.

Sand martin

Riparia riparia

SIZE AND DESCRIPTION 12 cm long. Small brown member of swallow family with white underparts, brown breast band, short forked tail.

VOICE Twittering song, not so musical as swallow.

HABITAT Open country with fresh water, rivers.

FOOD/HABITS Eats insects such as midges caught in flight. Nests colonially in holes in sandbanks. Summer visitor, on migration may roost in large numbers in reedbeds.

Skylark

Alauda arvensis

SIZE AND DESCRIPTION 18 cm long. Streaked brown upperparts, short crest not always obvious, white outer tail feathers. Walks rather than hops. Towering and hovering song flight.

VOICE Lengthy warbling song, delivered in flight as the bird rises vertically then drops through the air.

HABITAT Farmland, grassland, meadows and moorland.

FOOD/HABITS Eats insects, worms and seeds. Nests on the ground. Substantial decline in breeding population since 1970. Flocks in winter, when numbers swollen by European migrants.

Meadow pipit

Anthus pratensis

SIZE AND DESCRIPTION 14.5 cm long. Streaked brown upperparts; underparts more spotted. Darker legs than tree pipit.

VOICE Call "pheet" uttered once or three times. Song given in display flight as it describes an arc from the ground.

HABITAT Open country, heathland, moorland, grassland. May be seen in lowland or on coastlands in winter.

FOOD/HABITS Eats mostly insects, also spiders, earthworms and some seeds. Nests on the ground in a small depression.

Tree pipit

Anthus trivialis

SIZE AND DESCRIPTION 15 cm long. Similar to meadow pipit, but slightly stockier. Legs flesh pink. Walks rather than hops. Summer visitor.

VOICE Song shrill and musical, given in a flight from a tree, steeply ascending then parachuting down.

HABITAT Meadowland, heathland, with scattered trees.

FOOD/HABITS Diet is chiefly insects and spiders.

Pied/white wagtail

Motacilla alba

SIZE AND DESCRIPTION 17–19 cm long. The male of the British race (*M. yarrellii*) has a black back and wings, and the female a dark grey back. In the continental race, both male and female have a pale grey back. In flight, which is undulating, faint double wing bars can be seen. On the ground, the gait is rapid, with the head moving back and forth while wagging its tail.

VOICE Flight call is a "chissick", sometimes a "chissick-ick". Song is plain and twittery.

HABITAT Towns, gardens and open habitat. In winter pied wagtails roost in large flocks in warm places, such as around factories, and town centres.

FOOD/HABITS Runs rapidly after flying insects. Prefers feeding on lawns, roofs, car parks and roads, where prey is easily spotted.

Wren

Troglodytes troglodytes

SIZE AND DESCRIPTION 9–10 cm long. Its reddish-brown back is faintly barred, as are the paler flanks. There is a narrow dark eye-stripe, with a paler stripe above the eye. The bill is narrow, pointed and slightly downward-curving. The wren has a whirrring flight, like a large bee.

VOICE Calls are a repeated "tic-tic" and a metallic "clink". The song is a loud series of trills and warbles.

HABITAT Woodland with dense undergrowth, scrub, heathland, gardens, parks and moorland.

FOOD/HABITS Searches for insects and spiders on or near the ground, moving in a rather mouse-like way. During cold winter nights, flocks of wrens will roost together in a bundle.

Dunnock

Prunella modularis

SIZE AND DESCRIPTION 13–15 cm long. The streaking and brown colour of the dunnock give it a rather sparrow-like appearance, which is why it is often wrongly desribed as a hedge sparrow. Note the thin insect-picking bill, grey throat and face, and reddish-brown legs.

VOICE The alarm-call is a strong "tiih". The song is clear and quite loud.

HABITAT Gardens, parks, open woodland, heathland, farmland hedges over most of Europe.

FOOD/HABITS An unobtrusive bird that searches on the ground for seeds, berries, insects and other invertebrates.

Song thrush

Turdus philomelos

SIZE AND DESCRIPTION 20–22 cm long. The song thrush has a brown back and a speckled creamy breast (speckles are shaped like arrowheads, and more regular than those of the mistle thrush). In flight, underwings show yellowish-orange. Flies rather jerkily. Often sings at dusk.

VOICE A loud, strong song, with a variety of trilling and squeaky notes and frequent repetitions. The alarm call is a series of sharp, scolding notes

HABITAT Woodlands, parks and gardens.

FOOD/HABITS Feeds on worms, insects, berries and snails. Sometimes in small flocks.

Redwing

Turdus iliacus

SIZE AND DESCRIPTION 19–23 cm long. Similar size as a song thrush, but with a visibly larger head. The white stripe above the eye and the black-tipped yellow bill give it a striking appearance. The red patch under the wing is conspicuous when the bird flies. Flight is fast and direct.

VOICE A thin "tseep" contact call. The alarm call is hoarse and scolding. Song is variable, with loud fluted notes and prolonged twitters.

HABITAT Fields, open woodland, parks and gardens.

FOOD/HABITS Feeds on worms, insects and berries. Redwings are attracted to gardens by berry-bearing shrubs.

Fieldfare

Turdus pilaris

SIZE AND DESCRIPTION 22–27cm long. Smaller than the mistle thrush, but looks stockier. Has grey head, red-brown back and an apricot base to the speckled breast. Longish tail, pale grey rump and white underwings show clearly in flight. Rather flapping flight.

VOICE Call is a harsh "chack-chack-chack". The song is a tuneless, chattering babble.

HABITAT Open forest, town parks, fields and gardens.

FOOD/HABITS Feeds on worms, insects, berries and fruit. Fond of windfall fruits.

Mistle thrush

Turdus viscivorus

SIZE AND DESCRIPTION 22–27 cm long. This large thrush has an upright and comparatively longer tail than the song thrush. Its white breast is speckled with rounded, blotchy spots. In flight, the white outer tail feathers and narrow white wing-bars can be seen. The underwing is white. Stands in an upright posture. Flight is more undulating than the song thrush's.

VOICE Its flight call is a dry, churring rattle. Song is similar to the song thrush's.

HABITAT Woodland, parks, gardens.

FOOD/HABITS Eats worms, berries and insects. Will feed alongside other bird species.

Blackbird

Turdus merula

SIZE AND DESCRIPTION 23.5–29 cm long. The all-black male, with its yellow bill and yellow eye-ring, is unmistakable because it is larger and has a comparatively longer tail than the starling. The sooty-brown female, with a dark-streaked pale throat, and the gingery juveniles may be confused with other thrushes, but they have a solid build and cock their tails when landing. First-winter males have all-dark bills.

VOICE Alarm call is a harsh "chack-aack-aack-aack", or a series of high metallic notes when going to roost or when a cat is seen. The song is a rich, melodic fluting, often rising to a crescendo.

HABITAT Woodland, parks, orchards and gardens. Blackbirds in eastern Europe and Scandinavia migrate in winter.

FOOD/HABITS Hops or walks over the ground, stopping and cocking its head to look for worms or other food. Takes a wide range of food, including insects, worms, fruit and berries.

Black redstart

Pheonicurus ochruros

SIZE AND DESCRIPTION 14.5 cm long. Darker than redstart. Breeding male slaty-black above, with black face and breast and white flash in wing. Female duller brown. Reddish rump and tail in all plumages.

VOICE Song, a short high-pitched warble punctuated by characteristic gravelly notes. Call, a quiet "tsip-tsip".

HABITAT Towns, urban sites and cliffs.

FOOD/HABITS Eats mainly insects. Constantly shivers tail. Summer visitor to northern Europe. Rare breeder in south-east England.

Redstart

Phoenicurus phoenicurus

SIZE AND DESCRIPTION 14 cm long. Male has a grey back, black face and throat, white forehead. Bright chestnut breast and tail. Tail is waved up and down. Female is dull brown.

VOICE Calls "hooeet", and "kwee-tucc-tucc". Song, a squeaky warble.

HABITAT Usually deciduous upland woodland. Mature trees for nesting.

FOOD/HABITS Eats mainly insects, but also worms, spiders and berries.

Robin

Erithacus rubecula

SIZE AND DESCRIPTION 12.5–14 cm. The orange-red breast is fringed with pale grey. Note the pale wing-bar. Juvenile has a pale-spotted brown breast, and pale-flecked head and back.

VOICE The call is a short, hard repeated "tic". The alarm call is a thin, sharp "tsiih". The song is sweet, starting high, then a fall, then speeds up in clear notes.

HABITAT A woodland bird that breeds in gardens, parks and forest edges. In winter, northern European robins migrate south-west to southern Europe. Other populations are resident.

FOOD/HABITS Feeds on berries and insects on the ground. Moves over the ground by hopping vigorously.

Wheatear

Oenanthe oenanthe

SIZE AND DESCRIPTION 14.5 cm long. Summer visitor. Breeding male has blue-grey back, black eye mask, wings and lower tail; distinctive square white rump and upper tail visible in flight. Winter male is browner.

VOICE Call "chack, chack".

HABITAT Chiefly upland hills, pastures and cliffs; some lowland areas.

FOOD/HABITS Eats mostly insects. Nests on the ground, in rabbit burrows, holes under stones or in stone walls. An early spring migrant from March onwards.

juvenile

Stonechat

Saxicola torquata

SIZE AND DESCRIPTION 12.5 cm long. Male has black head, white patch on side of neck, white wingpatch, dark brown upper parts. Female is duller with streaked brown upper parts.

VOICE Call, persistent "tsak, tsak", like two stones being hit together. Plaintive song.

HABITAT Coastal heaths, especially with gorse, rough hillside grazing, upland moors.

FOOD/HABITS Diet is chiefly insects, also worms and spiders. Present all year. Nests on the ground often under cover of gorse bush.

Nightingale

Luscinia megarhynchos

SIZE AND DESCRIPTION 16.5 cm long. Summer visitor. Both male and female have russet-brown plumage with rufous tail. Skulking and secretive.

VOICE Loud melodious song uttered by day as well as late in the evening and early morning.

HABITAT Prefers lowland deciduous woodland, especially with coppice or with dense bushy undergrowth.

FOOD/HABITS Eats mostly insects and worms, but also takes fruit and berries.

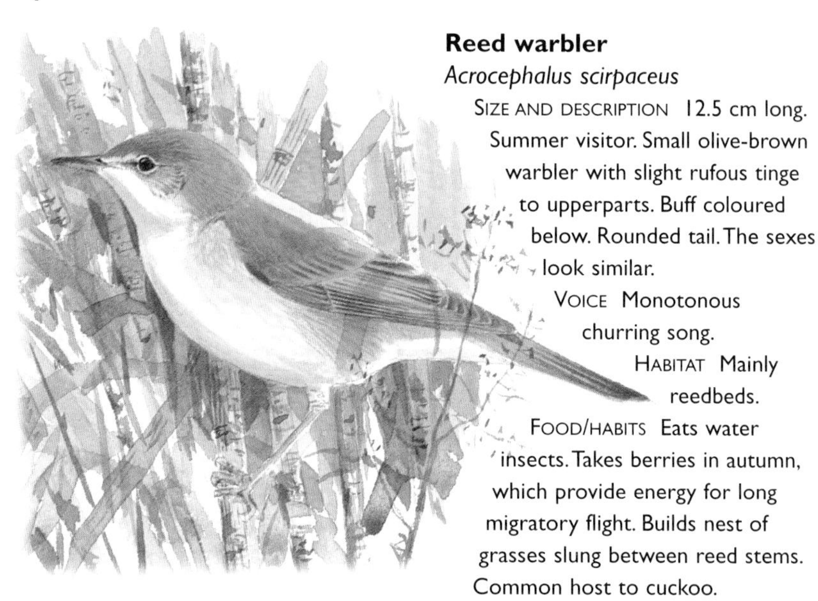

Reed warbler

Acrocephalus scirpaceus

SIZE AND DESCRIPTION 12.5 cm long. Summer visitor. Small olive-brown warbler with slight rufous tinge to upperparts. Buff coloured below. Rounded tail. The sexes look similar.

VOICE Monotonous churring song.

HABITAT Mainly reedbeds.

FOOD/HABITS Eats water insects. Takes berries in autumn, which provide energy for long migratory flight. Builds nest of grasses slung between reed stems. Common host to cuckoo.

Sedge warbler

Acrocephalus schoenobaenus

SIZE AND DESCRIPTION 13 cm long. Summer visitor. Olive-brown, streaked-backed warbler, with rounded tail and rufous-coloured rump. Conspicuous creamy-white stripe above eye. The sexes look similar.

VOICE Loud jumbly scratchy song.

HABITAT Waterside vegetation near reedbeds, rivers and lakes; lowland marsh, also dry scrubby areas.

FOOD/HABITS Chiefly eats insects; takes berries in autumn. Migrates to Africa in late summer. Nests in rank vegetation.

Whitethroat

Sylvia communis

SIZE AND DESCRIPTION 14 cm long. Summer visitor. Male has grey head, bright white throat, brown upperparts, pale under parts. Female has brown head. The tail is long and slim.

VOICE Call a sharp "tacc, tacc". Song is a rapid warble.

HABITAT Open woodland, gardens, hedgerows and scrub.

FOOD/HABITS Eats mainly insects; some fruits and berries in autumn. Nests in brambles, low bushes, not far from gound level.

Garden warbler

Sylvia borin

SIZE AND DESCRIPTION 14 cm long. Summer visitor. Inconspicuous little grey-brown warbler. Plumage uniform without any notable distinguishing feature. Round head, short bill.

VOICE Song most distinctive characteristic, a musical warble uttered from the depths of cover.

HABITAT Woodland; deciduous and mixed, with dense undergrowth.

FOOD/HABITS Eats mostly insects in early summer; also eats berries and other fruits before autumn migration. Nests in brambles and bushes.

Blackcap

Sylvia atricapilla

SIZE AND DESCRIPTION 14 cm long. Male has black cap; female's is red-brown. Cheeks are grey; upper parts dark grey-brown. Compare male with marsh and willow tits, which also have black caps.

VOICE Sweet, rich warbling song.

HABITAT Open woodland, shrubby areas with trees, gardens.

FOOD/HABITS Chiefly eats insects; berries and fruit are taken in late summer and autumn. Mostly a summer visitor to Great Britain, increasing numbers are seen in winter. Occasional visitor to bird tables.

Willow warbler

Phylloscopus trochilus

SIZE AND DESCRIPTION 11–12.5 cm long. The pale "eyebrow" (the supercilium) is its most obvious feature. The head, back and tail are generally brownish-green, and the throat and eyebrow are yellowish. Legs are usually pale brown. Primary feathers project beyond tertials.

VOICE The call is a soft "huitt", similar to the chiffchaff's. Song is rather sad.

HABITAT Upland birchwoods and other deciduous woods, as well as in parks and gardens.

FOOD/HABITS Small insects found among leaves.

Chiffchaff

Phylloscopus collybita

SIZE AND DESCRIPTION 10–12 cm long. Small, neat bird, with a fine bill and thin legs. Very similar to willow warbler. Primaries shorter. Legs are usually dark and the bill is even finer than the willow warbler's. The stripe above the eye is less distinct, while the darkish patch beneath the eye emphasises the white eye-ring.

VOICE The call is a soft "hueet", and the song is a distinctively slow "chiff-chaff-chiff-chaff".

HABITAT Open deciduous woodland with some scrub. Mainly a summer visitor to the British Isles, Scandinavia and central Europe.

FOOD/HABITS Similar to willow warbler.

Goldcrest

Regulus regulus

SIZE AND DESCRIPTION 8.5–9.5 cm long. This tiny bird has a greenish back, and a yellow crest that becomes orange in the male. The crest has a black stripe on each side. The face is greyish, with dark eyes surrounded by very pale grey.

VOICE A very high-pitched, thin call of three or four syllables: "see-see-see". Song is high-pitched and rhythmic, and ends with a trill.

HABITAT Coniferous and mixed woodlands. Goldcrests are often seen in yew and cypress trees.

FOOD/HABITS Tiny insects and spiders. The goldcrest feeds on the undersides of leaves.

Pied flycatcher

Ficedula hypoleuca

SIZE AND DESCRIPTION 12.5 cm. Breeding male has bold black-and-white plumage. Shorter tailed and more compact than spotted flycatcher, and distinguished in all plumages by white wingbar.

VOICE Song quite shrill "zee-it, zee-it", interspersed with trills. Calls include a metallic "whit".

HABITAT Deciduous, and sometimes coniferous forest.

FOOD/HABITS Summer visitor. Feeds on insects caught on the wing, and sometimes on the ground. Constantly flicking wings and tail. Keeps more to cover and seldom hunts from the same perch twice.

Spotted flycatcher

Muscicapa striata

SIZE AND DESCRIPTION 13.5–15 cm long. The back is greyish-brown with pale underparts, close examination reveals a streaked forehead and faintly streaked upper breast. Its bill and legs are black, and its black eye is an obvious feature. Upright posture when perched.

VOICE The call is a short, shrill "tzee". The song is quiet, simple and scratchy, often with soft trills.

HABITAT Open woodland and gardens.

FOOD/HABITS Flies up from perch to snatch flying insects, then returns to same spot.

Blue tit

Parus caeruleus

SIZE AND DESCRIPTION 11–12 cm long. Smaller than the great tit and possessing a bright blue crown. The stripe down the yellow breast is less well-defined than the great tit's. The tail and wings are blue. Young birds have yellow cheeks, and the blue parts are green.

VOICE A clear, ringing, high-pitched song, and a thin "see-see" call.

HABITAT Mixed and deciduous woodlands, parks and gardens. Found across Europe, except in Iceland and northern Norway.

FOOD/HABITS Feeds on insects, spiders and other small animals, finding them on tree branches and sometimes in the corners of windows. Often visits the bird table in winter. Feeds in flocks of up to 30 in winter, often with other species of tit.

Great tit

Parus major

SIZE AND DESCRIPTION

14 cm long. A black cap and a black stripe starting at the bill give the great tit a more ferocious expression than the blue tit. The male's breast-stripe becomes broader than the female's.

VOICE The great tit's rich and varied repertoire includes a metallic "pink" and a repeated "teacher-teacher".

HABITAT Woodlands and gardens. Many of the tits feeding in gardens in winter return to woods to feed in spring. Found across Europe, except in Iceland and northern Norway.

FOOD/HABITS Feeds on seeds and fruits. Also takes spiders and insect larvae in the breeding season. Eats sunflower seeds, peanuts, and fat at bird-tables.

Marsh tit

Parus palustris

SIZE AND DESCRIPTION 11.5 cm long. Very similar to willow tit, with large-headed, short-tailed appearance. But marsh tit has a shiny black cap, smaller black bib, and uniform wings.

VOICE Best distinguishing feature is call "pitchiuu". Song is a liquid bubbling sound.

HABITAT Mainly deciduous woodland, sometimes gardens.

FOOD/HABITS Diet is mainly insects, with seeds and berries, and beechmast, like other tits. Nests are made in tree holes, especially alder and willow.

Coal tit

Parus ater

SIZE AND DESCRIPTION 11.5 cm long. Smaller than the great tit, with a proportionately larger head. Black head has white cheeks, and there is a white patch on the nape. The back is grey and the breast is grey-brown. The double wing-bar shows in flight.

VOICE The most frequent call is a triple "tsee-tsee-tsee". The song is like a simpler, weaker great tit's song.

HABITAT Woodlands and gardens. Prefers coniferous trees. Found across Europe, except Iceland and northern Norway.

FOOD/HABITS Eats insects and seeds, particularly spruce cones in the north.

Long-tailed tit

Aegithalos caudatus

SIZE AND DESCRIPTION 12–14 cm long, including a tail that is at least as long as the dumpy body. With its pink, black and white body and long tail, the long-tailed tit is unmistakable.

VOICE A piercing, trisyllabic "tsee-tsee-tsee" call. Song similar to the blue tit's.

HABITAT Woods with bushy undergrowth, hedges and gardens.

FOOD/HABITS Feeds mainly on insects and small spiders, but is increasingly visiting bird-tables. Families form into flocks and move through woods and hedges, often with other tits.

Nuthatch

Sitta europaea

SIZE AND DESCRIPTION 12–14.5 cm long. Large head, lack of a neck, short tail and heavy pointed bill. The back and head are slate-grey, with a long black eye-stripe. The cheeks are white and the breast and underparts are rusty orange (darker in the male). In Scandinavian species, males have white breasts, females have pale orange. Flight similar to woodpecker's, but the tail-shape is rounded.

VOICE A loud, strident "hwitt" call. The song is a repetitive "peeu-peeu-peeu".

HABITAT Mixed, deciduous woods, parks and gardens with mature oaks. It is resident from western Russia across Europe. Absent from Ireland and Scotland.

FOOD/HABITS Feeds on nuts, seeds and invertebrates. Using its bill to winkle insects out of bark crevices.

Treecreeper

Certhia familiaris

SIZE AND DESCRIPTION 12.5–14 cm long. Mottled brown on the back and white on the underside makes excellent camouflage as it climbs tree-trunks. The fine bill curves downwards. The long, stiff tail helps the bird balance in an upright position against a trunk.

VOICE The call is a loud, thin "zzrreet". The song is several scratchy notes ending in a thin trill.

HABITAT Found in almost all woodland, parks, gardens and orchards with old trees with loose bark for nest-sites.

FOOD/HABITS The treecreeper probes bark crevices for insects and small spiders.

Starling

Sturnus vulgaris

SIZE AND DESCRIPTION 19–22 cm long. Superficially like a blackbird because of its black plumage and yellow bill. It has a short tail and neck, an upright stance, pink legs, white spots and a metallic green shine. In flight, has an arrowhead profile. Flocks fly in tight formation. Juveniles are grey brown.

VOICE A versatile mimic of other birds. Calls are creaky twitters, chirps, clicks and whistles.

HABITAT Widespread throughout Europe in all habitats, particularly human settlements.

FOOD/HABITS Berries, seeds and fruit. Roosts in huge flocks, favouring city buildings.

Magpie

Pica pica

SIZE AND DESCRIPTION 40–51 cm long, of which 20–30 cm is the tail. Wings are a metallic blue-black and the long, round-tipped tail has a metallic green sheen. Males are larger and tend to have longer tails than the females. Flight is often a series of jerky flaps interspersed with swooping glides.

VOICE The noisy alarm call is a staccato rattle. Other magpie sounds include a variety of bisyllabic calls.

HABITAT Breeds around farms and villages and in hedgerows. It is becoming increasingly common in urban areas. The magpie occurs throughout Europe, except in Iceland, northernmost Scotland and the far north of Norway.

FOOD/HABITS The magpie is an omnivore that feeds on seeds, insects, carrion (it is often seen feeding on roadside casualties), nestlings and eggs.

Rook

Corvus frugilegus

SIZE AND DESCRIPTION 46 cm long. Large black bird with "ragged trousered" appearance. Bare face patch makes bill seem very long. Purple-gloss to plumage. Juvenile has all-dark face.

VOICE Wide variety of calls, including harsh "caw".

HABITAT Farmland, both pasture and arable, with trees for nesting.

FOOD/HABITS Eats mostly vegetable matter, seeds, roots, cereals and fruits. Also takes variety of animal food.

Carrion crow

Corvus corone

SIZE AND DESCRIPTION 44–51 cm long. Carrion crow is totally black, with a stout bill. The hooded crow, the subspecies found in eastern and northern Europe, has grey underparts and a grey back. In flight, the wingbeats are shallow and the tail is rounded.

VOICE A hard, rolling "krra-kra-kraa".

HABITAT A wide variety of habitats, from the coast to the mountains.

FOOD/HABITS An omnivore, this crow feeds on carrion, nestlings and eggs, grain and insects. Tends to be less sociable than the rook.

Jay

Garrulus glandarius

SIZE AND DESCRIPTION 32–35 cm long. The streaked feathers on the forehead are often raised in a crest. The jay has a pale eye, a black moustache and a blue-and-black wing-flash. White rump obvious in flight.

VOICE The call is a noisy, screeching "kscharch".

HABITAT Wherever plentiful supply of acorns.

FOOD/HABITS Seeds, fruits, bird eggs, nestlings, insects. Buries acorns and beechnuts.

Jackdaw

Corvus monedula

SIZE AND DESCRIPTION 30–34 cm long. Its nape is grey and its eye has a very pale iris. Struts as it walks. In flight, the wing-beats are faster and deeper than the crow's. It flies in flocks almost as densely as pigeons.

VOICE Calls are a metallic, high-pitched "kya" and "chak".

HABITAT Found throughout Europe.

FOOD/HABITS Omnivorous, the jackdaw will eat invertebrates, eggs, nestlings and grain.

Chaffinch

Fringilla coelebs

SIZE AND DESCRIPTION 14–16 cm long. In winter, the blue-grey of the head and pink of the breast are subdued. The female is most likely to be confused with the female house sparrow. Two white bars on each wing can be seen during the chaffinch's strong undulating flight.

VOICE The call is a sharp "pink", but the flight call is a softer "yupp". The song is a loud, ringing trill that becomes lower, then ends in a flourish, then repeated.

HABITAT This very common bird breeds in all types of woodland, as well as in parks and gardens. Flocks form in autumn. British chaffinches are resident, but birds from elsewhere in Europe may winter in Britain.

FOOD/HABITS Eats fruits and seeds, and also takes insects during breeding season.

Bullfinch

Pyrrhula pyrrhula

SIZE AND DESCRIPTION 15.5–17.5 cm long. A compact, bull-necked finch, with a black cap. The male has a rosy red breast, grey back, white rump and black tail. The female has a pale brown breast. Juveniles have grey-brown heads and breast-colour. Both sexes have white wing-bars that show in flight. Flight is fast and gently undulating.

VOICE Call is a soft, sad fluted whistle.

HABITAT Mixed woodland, parks, large gardens and churchyards. Feeds in orchards and gardens.

FOOD/HABITS Buds and seeds and insects in the breeding season.

Hawfinch

Coccothraustes coccothraustes

SIZE AND DESCRIPTION 16.5–18 cm long. Big head, huge bill and short tail. The bill is blueish-black in summer, becoming brown in winter. Male's flight feathers are black, the female's secondaries are grey. In flight, white wing-bars are visible.

VOICE A sharp, "tic". The song is a soft, series of "zih" and "zri" notes.

HABITAT Deciduous and mixed woodland.

FOOD/HABITS Seeds, cherry-stones and nuts.

Greenfinch

Carduelis chloris

SIZE AND DESCRIPTION 14–16 cm long. In summer, adults are olive-green, merging into grey-green on the face, wings and flanks, with bright yellow wing feathers on either side of the tail. The female's colouring is subdued. The juvenile is paler and even more streaked. Flight is bouncing and undulating.

VOICE Flight call is a sharp "burrurrup". Song is a wheezy sequence of twitters and whistles.

HABITAT Breeding habitats comprise woodland edges, open woodland, parks, gardens and farmland with hedges. In winter, flocks may be seen feeding in farmland and gardens.

FOOD/HABITS Seeds and berries, along with some insects during the breeding season. A visitor to garden bird-tables.

Serin

Serinus serinus

SIZE AND DESCRIPTION 11.5 cm long. Small finch. Male is yellow-green with dark streaks, bright yellow head and breast, yellow rump. Female rather duller. Short bill.

VOICE Song has a jingling quality.

HABITAT Gardens, parks, churchyards.

FOOD/HABITS Mostly eats plant seeds, also alder and birch seeds. Breeds in extremely small numbers, mostly Devon, Dorset and East Anglia, in the UK, and southern Europe.

Siskin

Carduelis spinus

SIZE AND DESCRIPTION 11–12.5 cm long. Dark-streaked, greenish-yellow plumage. The male is yellower than the female, and has a black cap and bib. Wing-bars in both sexes are yellow, and the male's tail has yellow patches on either side. Tails are deeply notched. Flight is flitting and uneven.

VOICE The flight call is either a descending "tilu" or a rising "tlui". Twittery, trilling song.

HABITAT Coniferous and mixed forests.

FOOD/HABITS Seeds of trees.

Linnet

Carduelis cannabina

SIZE AND DESCRIPTION 13.5 cm long. In breeding plumage, male has crimson forehead and breast, chestnut mantle. Winter males resemble females, which lack the pink markings.

VOICE Song a pleasant twitter.

HABITAT Commons and rough grounds in summer, with bushes and scrub. Farmland and coasts in winter.

FOOD/HABITS Mostly eats seeds and arable weeds.

Redpoll

Carduelis flammea

SIZE AND DESCRIPTION 11.5–14 cm long. Greyish-brown and dark-streaked colouring. The bill is small and broad. Both sexes have a red forehead and a small black bib. The adult male has a red upper breast. The wings are dark, with faint wing-bars. Juveniles lack red head.

VOICE Flight call is a hard metallic "chet-chet-chet".

HABITAT Conifers, birch forest, willows and copses.

FOOD/HABITS Feeds in flocks, searching among the tips of birch trees for seeds. Visits gardens in winter.

Goldfinch

Carduelis carduelis

SIZE AND DESCRIPTION 12–13.5 cm long. Red face, white cheeks and throat, black cap and black-and-gold wings. In flight, the wings show broad golden bands, and the white rump and black tail are visible. Sexes alike, but juveniles have a brown-streaked head.

VOICE A cheerful trisyllabic "tickelitt" call. Song has a series of rapid trills and twitters.

HABITAT Open lowland woodland, heaths, orchards and gardens.

FOOD/HABITS Seeds and berries. Especially teasels and thistleheads.

Yellowhammer

Emberiza citrinella

SIZE AND DESCRIPTION 16.5 cm long. Male has vivid yellow head, brown streaked back and chestnut rump. Female is more dull. White outer tail feathers.

VOICE Song is a jingling phrase on one note "little bit of bread and no cheese".

HABITAT Arable farmland grassland, with banks or hedges. In winter flocks to feed in stubblefields and farmyards.

FOOD/HABITS Grasses, seeds, fruits and insects.

Corn bunting

Miliaria calandra

SIZE AND DESCRIPTION 18 cm long. Large, plain bunting, brown with dark streaks. No white markings.

VOICE Distinctive, jangling monotonous song is high-pitched, likened to keys being jingled.

HABITAT Farmland, arable and grassland, with bushes and hedges.

FOOD/HABITS Mostly eats seeds, corn, fruits and other vegetable matter, also insects and earthworms. Very sedentary. Sings from a prominent perch.

Tree sparrow

Passer montanus

SIZE AND DESCRIPTION 14 cm long. The sexes look similar. Distinguished from male house sparrow by chestnut crown and nape, white cheeks, small neat black bib, black spot behind the eye.

VOICE Song more musical than that of house sparrow.

HABITAT Farmland and suburbs, but not a town bird. In winter flocks to feed in stubblefields with finches and buntings. Growing scarce in Britain.

FOOD/HABITS Diet is mostly weed seeds and corn, also insects and spiders. Nests in holes in trees.

House sparrow

Passer domesticus

SIZE AND DESCRIPTION 14–16 cm long. The male has a grey cap and grey breast, with an extensive black throat-patch. The female has a pale brown cap and buff eye-stripe. Wings of both sexes have small white wing-bars.

VOICE Monotonous chirps.

HABITAT Completely linked to humans. It is found in towns, villages and farmland near human habitation. In winter, flocks can be seen feeding in fields.

FOOD/HABITS An omnivore that feeds on seeds and insects, as well as bread and other food left by people.

Addresses

British Trust for Ornithology
The Nunnery
Thetford
Norfolk IP24 2PU
Tel 01842 750050
Fax 01842 750030
E-mail info@bto.org
Website www.bto.org

RSPB
The Lodge
Sandy
Bedfordshire SG19 2DL
Tel 01767 680551
Fax 01767 692365
E-mail bird@rspb.demon.co.uk
Website www.rspb.org.uk

The Wildlife Trusts
The Kiln, Waterside
Mather Road
Newark
Nottinghamshire NG24 1WT
Tel 0870 036 7711
Fax 0870 036 0101
E-mail info@wildlife-trusts.cix.co.uk
Website www.wildlifetrusts.org

Wildlife Watch
(Contact details as above)
E-mail watch@wildlife-trusts.cix.co.uk

CJ Wildbird Foods
The Rea
Upton Magna
Shrewsbury SY4 4UB
Tel 0800 7312820
Fax 01743 709504
E-mail sales@birdfood.co.uk
Website www.birdfood.co.uk

Birdguides
Videos, CDs, CD-Roms
Tel 0800 919391
Website www.birdguides.com

Garden Bird Supplies
Wem
Shrewsbury
Shropshire SY4 5BF
E-mail info@gardenbird.com
Website www.gardenbird.com

Binoculars & telescopes
In Focus
Website www.at-infocus.co.uk
(Branches in Hertfordshire, London, Norfolk, West Yorkshire, Rutland, Gloucestershire, Lancashire.)

NHBS
2–3 Wills Road
Totnes
Devon TQ9 5XN
Tel 01803 865913
E-mail nhbs@nhbs.co.uk
Website www.nhbs.com

Suggested reading

Brooke, Michael & Birkhead, Tim
Cambridge Encyclopedia of Ornithology
Cambridge University Press, 1991

Burton, Robert
Birdfeeder Handbook
Dorling Kindersley, 1991

Golley, M., Moss, S. & Daly, D.
The Complete Garden Bird Book
New Holland, 1998

Hammond, Nicholas & Pearson, Bruce
The Birds in Your Garden
Hamlyn, 1995

Jonsson, Lars
Birds of Europe
Helm, 1992

Moss, Stephen & Cottridge, David
Attracting Birds to Your Garden
New Holland, 1997

Mullarney, K., Svensson, K.,
Zetterstrom, D. & Grant, P.
Collins Field Guide to the Birds of Britain and Europe
Harper Collins, 1999

Oddie, Bill
Introduction to Birdwatching
New Holland, 2002

Packham, Chris
Chris Packham's Back Garden Nature Reserve
New Holland & The Wildlife Trusts, 2001

Index

Common names

Scientific names